S.O.S. Saving Our Students

A Collaborative Approach to Intervention

By: Dr. Donisha N. Bailey

S.O.S. Saving Our Students

A Collaborative Approach to Intervention

Special thanks to: Monique Reddix, Donovan Boyd, Sr., and The Boyd Group team for their support throughout the process of creating this book.

Cover Illustration and Design by: Austin Sims, Design World

Published by: The Boyd Group, LLC Publishing

Ordering and Booking Information: For ordering details or to book Dr. Bailey for your next speaking engagement, please contact: drdonishabailey@gmail.com

Special discounts may be available on large quantity purchases of book by corporations, associations, etc.

1st Edition

ISBN: 978-1-7321743-2-0 (print)

Dedication

This book is dedicated to all educational professionals who are passionate about meeting the needs of students, but who are not equipped with the tools needed to collaborate effectively with other educators, and/or to work in inclusive classroom settings. This book is also dedicated to every student who is struggling to be successful.

Table of Contents

About the Author

Dr. Donisha N. Bailey is a mother of one, and was born and raised in East Cleveland, Ohio. She is an Intervention Specialist, and the founder of The Literacy Club with Dr. Bailey, a non-profit organization that promotes literacy through writing, speaking, and listening skills. Dr. Bailey earned a Bachelor's Degree from Case Western Reserve University, a Master's Degree in Special Education from Notre Dame College, and a Doctorate Degree from Walden University in Educational Administration. She is currently entering her final semester in the Inspired Leaders Principal Program at Cleveland State University.

Over the last 7 years Dr. Bailey has served in both the charter and public-school settings in which she has taught grades 2-5 and 9-12. She has also served as a Dean of Student Life and Management. Currently, Dr. Bailey is an Intervention Specialist in the Euclid City School District, adjunct professor, and columnist for the East Clevelander, and a member of The National Society of Leadership and Success.

Dr. Bailey is the author of the book S.O.S. Saving Our Students: A Collaborative Approach to Intervention, a tool created to emphasize the importance of collaboration in inclusive classrooms, and the professional development sessions that are needed to assist educators in providing high quality instruction. Dr. Bailey is passionate about working in the community, and saving our students by tailoring lessons to their needs, through differentiation, small group instruction, collaboration, and professional development.

Introduction

"Education is the most powerful weapon which you can use to change the world."

-President Nelson Mandela

Each year there are more students who are diagnosed with a range of disabilities who become part of inclusive classroom settings. According to inclusion statistics from the U.S. Department of Education, students who have been diagnosed with a disability, and who are being educated in inclusive settings has double from 1989-2017. Inclusive classes contain students with and without disabilities who are educated together in the same setting. In order to save our students there needs to be a collaborative effort of educational professionals to differentiate lessons, and provide interventions to meet the needs of all students.

Collaboration amongst educators is a key factor for students to increase achievement in the inclusive setting. However, not all teacher preparation programs equipped educators with the tools they needed to effectively collaborate with other educators, or to work in inclusive classroom settings. This causes a gap in the knowledge that educators need to have in order to provide high quality instruction to students who are in inclusive classroom settings.

In order to close this gap it is the responsibility of administration to provide professional development opportunities according to the needs of educators. Not only do administrators have the responsibility of equipping educators with the skills that they need to teach effectively in inclusive classroom settings, they are also responsible for making sure that education laws are being followed to protect students' rights. In an effort to make sure that legal documents and other laws are being followed there are certain professional development sessions that should be required, in addition to the other sessions that are needed to meet the personalized needs of educators, as much as possible.

There should be professional development sessions that are based on 6 different categories: inclusive pedagogy, collaboration and time management, response to intervention, modifications and accommodations, self-efficacy and emotional intelligence, and connecting and collaborating with the community. It is important to understand each of these topics in order to give students the knowledge that they need, and to follow legal documents that some students have who are a part of inclusive classes.

Additionally, some of these sessions will require follow-up sessions according to the needs of the educators who are being trained. However, educators have to be willing to be professionally developed, they must have a positive attitude towards inclusive education, and develop a high sense of self-efficacy. All of these factors directly affect the effectiveness of instruction, and how inclusive practices are executed. When teachers are supported by administration through professional development sessions they tend to have a more positive attitude towards inclusion and they have a higher sense of self-efficacy, which will positively affect inclusive practices.

Saving our students is more than educators being professionally developed to work in inclusive classroom settings. Saving our students is more than adopting an inclusive pedagogy, and collaborating with other educators. Saving our students is more than educators having emotional intelligence. Saving our students in more than building rapport with students, their families, and the rest of the community.

Saving our students is a combination of each of these entities with the joint support and effort of administrators, and the willingness and effort of educators. Saving our students is a journey that interventionists, general education teachers, paraprofessionals, and administrators have to take together with the same end goal in mind, increasing student achievement through collaborative efforts. Saving our students is a movement. Saving our students is a collaborative approach to intervention.

Chapter 1

Inclusive Education and Co-Teaching Models

"Collaboration, creativity, and respect build life long connections that matter and make a difference, propelling us to work together across all boundaries."

-Diane Luna

The number of students who are being diagnosed with a disability has been on the rise in the United States of America for decades, according to statistics from the U.S. Department of Education, which has led to an increase in inclusive education. These students begin learning from the Common Core Standards. The Common Core Standards Initiative was created by the U.S. Department of Education in 2010, and it details the content that students in grades K-12 should know, regarding English Language Arts and Mathematics, throughout the United States.

According to The Common Core Standards Initiative (2020), the Common Core Program is a voluntary program for states to adopt, which was fully implemented during the 2013-2014 academic school year. However by 2017, forty-one states, the

Department of Education Activity, the District of Columbia, and four territories have adopted these academic standards. When educators begin to notice that students are having difficulty mastering these standards, they implement Response to Intervention to provide small group instruction and targeted interventions. At the end of this process students may or may not need testing to see if they qualify for special education services.

Students who have been diagnosed with a disability either have a document called an Individualized Education Program (IEP), or they have a 504 plan written for them that is good for 1 year minus 1 day (364 days). An IEP is an individualized educational plan written by the Intervention Specialist (IS), with input from other members of the IEP team. Required members of an IEP team include the IS, a general education teacher, a district representative or administrator, and a parent/guardian. However, some students may require additional services such as speech or occupational therapy.

In these cases a Speech and Language Pathologist (SLP), and/or an Occupational Therapist (OT) are members of the IEP team as well. The IEP contains goals and objectives for the student during this time, as well as accommodations and modifications that are needed to help students successfully access the curriculum. There is also a section that discusses specially designed instruction, which documents the person who is responsible for the instruction, the location, and the amount of time that will be spent on working on specific goals. For example, a student with a math goal may have 60 minutes per week in which he/she works in the resource room with the IS.

While a 504 Plan does not contain goals and objectives, it does contain modifications and/or accommodations for students. A student may be diagnosed with a disability, such as Attention Deficit Hyperactivity Disorder (ADHD), and may not qualify for an IEP, but he/she may qualify for a 504 plan because the requirements are broader, and only require the factor that impedes learning. An example of this would be if a student is diagnosed with ADHD, he/she might be able to perform on grade level if their seat is moved to the front of the classroom to help him/her focus.

The 504 team includes fewer members: the school Principal, the parent/guardian, and the general education teacher. Both an IEP and a 504 Plan are legal documents that must be followed by every educator who students work with in the inclusive classroom setting.

Inclusive classroom environments contain students, with and without disabilities, who are being educated together. However, inclusive education can look, sound, and feel differently depending on the school, the diverse abilities of the students, as well as the number of students and teachers who are in the classroom.

There are different inclusive classroom settings that may be present in the general education classroom that consists of general education teachers and Intervention Specialists (IS) or interventionists, and within this, there are several co-teaching models that can be used to save our students. There are also push-in and pull-out services in which the IS visits the classroom to observe the content that the teacher is teaching, to help students, and to take students to the resource room to reteach lessons. Pull-out services are not only used for re-teaching, but these services are also used for working on specific goals and objectives that are in students' IEPs. The IS also provides this specially designed instruction (SDI) within the inclusive classroom setting.

The next educational setting that will be discussed is not a part of inclusive education; it is actually the opposite, self-contained classroom, or single classroom environments. Sometimes saving our students means that they need to be educated in a self-contained environment. However, while self-contained environments are settings in which only students with disabilities are educated, it is important to touch on the fact that there is still a need for collaboration with other teachers, interventionists, or paraprofessionals.

Different Ways to Educate Students with Disabilities

Inclusive education looks different across the country, within different states, within a district, and within a school from grade level to grade level, from classroom to classroom. As an interventionist, I have had the privilege of working in classrooms in different capacities. I have provided push-in and pull-out services, I have been a part of different co-teaching models with general education teachers (1, 2, and 3 teachers at a time), and I have taught in a self-contained classroom environment.

Each experience was different according to the needs of the students, the teachers who I worked with, and the number of teachers that I had to work with throughout the school year. However, one entity that was constant was our efforts to work to save our students by increasing student achievement.

Self-contained Classroom Environment

A self-contained classroom environment is the opposite of an inclusive classroom setting because self-contained classes only contain students with disabilities. However, it is important to collaborate with general education teachers so that educators are still providing students with grade level texts, but in a tailored fashion. It is also important to collaborate with paraprofessionals, or education assistants, because they are working with the same students, and together there can be a plan set to address the needs of the students.

When I was an IS in a self-contained classroom I taught reading, writing, math, science, social studies, and a life skills classes to students in grades 9-12. While most of their abilities varied from grade level K-6, I still met with other content teachers, and I observed some of their classes to see what students in inclusive classroom settings were learning. However, we did not officially collaborate. I did not have the same lunch or planning periods as most of the general education teachers, so there was not much time for collaboration. When I did speak with them, or sat in on one of their classes it was during my lunch and/or planning period. Every Friday we had professional development sessions or staff meetings, but this was not an opportunity to collaborate.

There were four paraprofessionals in the class that supported both the students and myself, as the interventionist, and I collaborated with them on a daily basis. We all valued one another's advice and professional opinions. We respected one another, and ultimately our goal was to increase student achievement and confidence. We collaborated whenever the opportunity presented itself because paraprofessionals did not have planning periods.

Push-in and Pull-out Services

When I provided push-in and pull-out services in inclusive classroom settings, I would observe what the teachers were teaching for that day during direct instruction, and when the students began to work in small groups, or independently I would pull the students with disabilities (SWD) out of the classroom, and take them to the resource room to work on the goals and objectives in their IEP. I would also reteach whatever concepts they did not grasp from the lesson in class. However, there was no collaboration between myself, and the general education teachers. The main issue was time. When interventionists work with different teachers and/or different grade levels, then they do not have the same planning period as all teachers, which leaves no time to collaborate. When we did communicate it was mostly through email, but even that was not often.

Co-Teaching within Inclusive Classroom Settings

As an interventionist in a co-teaching inclusive classroom environment, collaboration occurred daily because we shared the same planning and lunch periods. Not only did we have the same lunch and planning periods, we also had weekly Teacher Based Team (TBT) meetings, and one staff meeting, every other month, was designated for TBT as well. However, even though this time was made available, my co-teaching experiences varied based upon the different teachers, and the amount of teachers that I had to work with.

My first year co-teaching as an interventionist in an inclusive classroom environment was the best experience that I have had in a co-teaching environment that consisted of an interventionist and a general education teacher. I co-taught with two teachers that year, one teacher taught reading and social studies, and the other teacher taught mathematics and science. I worked with the reading teacher to find specific books based on students' grade levels, and we found materials and interventions and shared them with one another, but we did not actually plan together, even though we had the same planning period.

However, I did collaborate daily with the mathematics teacher. Not only did we have the same lunch and planning periods, we had the same class for homeroom. So, we had almost an extra hour together than the other teachers and I had. The extra time that we had together to collaborate made our instruction more effective and even stronger.

Co-Teaching

Co-teaching in an inclusive classroom setting consists of a general education teacher, who is an expert in the content, and an IS who is an expert in providing interventionists for students with disabilities to be successful with the curriculum in the classroom, which follows Common Core State Standards. However, interventionists also have to take content assessments for the state that they work in as well. In order to provide the appropriate intervention an IS should also be experts in the process of learning, and they must know the content, which can be a limiting factor for some interventionists.

In order for me to become a licensed Intervention Specialist for grades K-12, I had to take two assessments. I had to take an assessment that tested my knowledge of special education, and I had to take an assessment on K-12 education. I also completed a reading endorsement program with my Master's Degree, so I took a third assessment so that I would be endorsed in reading. However as stated above, knowing the content can be a limiting factor for some individuals because there is more of a focus on special education in teacher programs that prepare you to be an interventionist.

I had the privilege of working as a general education co-teacher alongside a licensed teacher during my first 2 years in the classroom, in both 2nd and 5th grades. At this point I was still in school obtaining my degree in special education, and I had no prior degree in education. I did have experience as a daycare teacher and Director, and I obtained a certificate from Cuyahoga Community College to do so, in between my Bachelor's and Master's programs. However, in most charter school settings, if you have a Bachelor's degree, in just about anything, you are able to co-teach with a licensed teacher.

Throughout my co-teaching experience I learned a lot from collaborating with educators, especially during my first two years as a general education co-teacher. Even after my teacher preparation program, and obtaining my teaching license, I learned a lot about academic content through co-teaching. I may know how to solve a problem, or the answer to a question, but knowing how to teach it to students to develop a true meaning is different. I was an expert at finding interventions for students to become successful in the classroom, and although I passed my K-12 Ohio Educator Assessment, I was no expert in academic content. I became an expert by working with the state standards to create lesson plans from scratch, co-teaching with different teachers, and putting research-based instructional strategies in motion. Co-teaching and collaborating with other educators played a tremendous role in my overall success as an educator.

Within the co-teaching model there are sub-models. According to the Academy of Co-teaching and Collaboration, these sub-models include: One Teach One Support, Parallel Teaching, Alternative Teaching, Station Teaching, and Team Teaching. Each of these co-teaching models can be used with two general education teachers; however, in an inclusive classroom setting there is usually a teacher and an interventionist. Each of these models that are addressed will be in reference to an inclusive classroom setting that educates students with and without disabilities, that consists of a teacher and an interventionist.

One Teach, One Support

The One Teach, One Support co-teaching model is when the teacher is teaching, and the interventionist is circulating around the room, assisting and observing students. For example, while the teacher is using direct instruction to introduce a math lesson, the interventionist is circulating making sure that students are taking notes, and that they are paying attention to the lesson. Then when a teacher models how to complete certain math equations, and students are working independently, the teacher is circulating with the interventionist to clear up any misconceptions.

Some of the advantages to this co-teaching model are students are able to obtain immediate feedback from the interventionist who is circulating and addressing students' misconceptions, and students stay on task for the most part. Some of the disadvantages of this co-teaching model are some students could be distracted with a person circulating around the room, and students could get used to one-on-one assistance and immediate feedback, but may not always receive it in the future.

Parallel Co-Teaching

The parallel co-teaching model is when teachers plan together, and they split the class in half to teach the same content. For example, if there is a reading lesson about making inferences, one teacher will arrange for half of the class to be turned in a certain direction to receive instruction, and the interventionist will do the same with the other half of the class. Some teachers will bring the class back together as a whole at the end of the lesson to recap what was taught, and/or to take a formative assessment, such as an exit slip, to check for understanding.

Some of the advantages to the parallel co-teaching model are; teachers get a chance to plan together, teachers can work with smaller groups of students, and splitting the class can allow teachers to focus more on the individual needs of students. Some of the disadvantages to this co-teaching model are; some teachers are going to have to keep the same pace of the lesson, and there has to be a controlled voice level so that the groups are not disturbing one another.

Alternative Co-Teaching

The Alternative Co-teaching model is when one teacher manages most of the class, and the other teacher works in small groups, inside or outside of the classroom. In this case the interventionist would be the person taking students in a small group. More than likely the interventionist would only take students to the resource room who have an IEP. However, the small groups within the classroom could contain students with or without an IEP.

Some of the advantages to alternative teaching are students who do not have disabilities are able to receive interventions in small groups, students who do have disabilities are able to get a lesson retaught to them, and they are able to work on their goals and objectives that are present in their IEPs. Some of the disadvantages to this co-teaching model are there must be adequate space for small groups within the classroom, the groups also should not be labeled as high, medium, or low (use colors), because students will begin labeling a group as the smart group, and this could affect students self-confidence.

Station Teaching

Station Teaching is a co-teaching model in which the instructional content is divided, and the teacher and the interventionist are responsible for teaching different parts of the lesson. The idea is that the class is set up in stations, and one station is being taught by the teacher, another station is being taught by the interventionist, and the other stations are designated for independent learning.

When I was a second grade teacher we conducted different types of co-teaching models in one day. We would use a version of Boushey & Moser's Daily 5, in which there was a focus of teaching, learning independence, and stamina. Our version of the Daily 5 included five stations that were set up around the room, and students would rotate to each station during their reading block.

We put a twist on it and we had one group of students on the computer working on iReady, an online diagnostic assessment and learning path for students in reading and math. There was another group who was working independently on vocabulary (such as rainbow art). Another group working on answering writing prompts, and the other two groups would each work with an educator. However, this was my first year as a teacher, and most of the time my co-teacher would teach the main lesson in her group, and I would reteach or review in my groups. The groups would rotate every 25 minutes.

Some of the advantages to station teaching are; each educator has clear responsibilities, students can work in small groups, and more material can be covered in a smaller amount of time. Some of the disadvantages to station teaching are the stations must be paced so that all of the groups end on time, there is a lot of pre-planning that needs to be done to execute this effectively, the noise level must be maintained so distractions are at a minimum, and students have to build stamina in order to work independently without interrupting teachers while they are working in a small group.

Team Teaching

Team teaching is a co-teaching model in which both educators are responsible for planning lessons and instructing students. For example, a teacher and an interventionist could plan a science lesson together, and they could each deliver diverse parts of the lesson. The lesson could be on states of matter, and the teacher could focus on liquids, the interventionist could focus on solids, and they both could discuss gasses. However they decide to do it, educators are executing the lesson delivery as a team.

Some of the advantages to team teaching are; both teachers have active roles in the classroom, teachers are more likely to try new entities in a team rather than alone, and teachers have a chance to collaborate. Some of the disadvantages to team teaching are; there is a lot of pre-planning that needs to occur, and educator's roles should be clearly defined so that their shared responsibility is truly equal.

Putting it all Together

Each of the mentioned co-teaching models allow teachers and interventionists to work collaboratively in inclusive classroom settings. As a previous general education co-teacher, and as an interventionist who is currently in a co-teaching model with teachers, there have been times when teachers and I have used multiple teaching models in one day in order to address students' specific needs and to save all of our students. In inclusive classroom settings, there are students who have a range of abilities and diverse learning needs and styles. In regard to instructional practices, co-teaching models and collaboration need to take place to save our students.

However, regardless of the inclusive classroom environment that educators are a part of, or the co-teaching model that is being used, what is ultimately important is collaborating with one another for the increased success of students.

Things to Remember

■ There is an increase in the demand of inclusive classroom environments because there is an increase in students who have been diagnosed with a disability.

■ SWD are either educated in inclusive classrooms or self-contained environments.

■ Co-teaching models

  ○ One Teach, One Support

  ○ Parallel Teaching

  ○ Alternative Teaching

  ○ Station Teaching

  ○ Team Teaching

■ Regardless of the inclusive classroom environment, the self-contained environment, or the co-teaching style that is being used, collaboration amongst educators is key in increasing student achievement.

Chapter 2

Teacher Preparation Programs and Professional Development

"The progress of the world will call for the best that all of us have to give."

-Mary McLeod Bethune

S tudents who are educated in inclusive classrooms need to have professionals who are experts in inclusive practices so that they can increase their achievement. According to Zagona (2017), when students are receiving high quality instruction through inclusive practices, their achievement increases. Teacher preparation programs are directly related to professional development (PD) sessions for both novice and veteran teachers.

PD sessions should not be limited to interventionists and teachers, but they should include paraprofessionals as well because they too work with students in inclusive classroom settings. The collaborative efforts of all of these professionals are needed to save our students.

Teacher Preparation Programs

There is a lack of preparation regarding collaboration and educating students in inclusive classroom environments, amongst novice and veteran educators. Novice educators are not being taught how to collaborate with other educators in inclusive classroom settings. Instead there is a focus on how to write IEPs, which is very important. There is also a focus on modifications and accommodations, the diverse disabilities that students may have, and interventions that could work.

All of these entities that were present in my teacher preparation program were well needed and amazing, and each of them helped shape the professional that I am today. However, there is still a need for educating teachers and interventionists on how to work together within an inclusive setting. Also, there is a need to educate these professionals on how to collaborate successfully with other educators in order to increase student achievement.

Many veteran teachers are lacking in how to educate students in inclusive classrooms as well as how to collaborate with other educators. This is in part, due to the nonexistence of inclusive settings when many veteran educators attended college. In the past, students who were diagnosed as having disabilities were educated in self-contained environments, which means they were not educated in a classroom with the general education population. Due to the lack of preparation to work in inclusive classroom settings, the lack of guidance on how to collaborate for novice teachers, and the lack of inclusive education settings when veteran teachers were in college, professional development sessions are needed to fill the gaps in knowledge that exist where educators are lacking.

According to Blanton & Juma (2017), in order for inclusive classroom settings to be successful teacher education reform needs to take place. Part of this is having adequate PDs available for educators. Training educators is a huge part of successful inclusion and collaboration. PDs are necessary because education is forever changing. Shaffer and Thomas-Brown (2015) explain how ongoing professional development is important in order to keep educators current on educational practices and information.

Diverse Professional Development Sessions

While PD sessions should be tailored to the needs of educators, there are some PD sessions that are necessary for educators to attend in an effort to save our students. The six (6) areas in which teachers and interventionists, and other professionals who

work in inclusive classroom settings, need additional training/
professional development in include:

1. Inclusive Pedagogy
2. Collaboration and Time Management
3. Response to Intervention
4. Modifications and Accommodations
5. Self-efficacy and Emotional Intelligence
6. Connecting with the community

Inclusive Pedagogy

Educators who work in inclusive classroom settings should adopt
an inclusive pedagogy. Mintz & Wyse (2015) describe an inclusive
pedagogy as one that contains inclusive practices, and enables
teachers to deliver lessons that meet the needs of all students. This
student-centered teaching style requires instructional practices to
be planned in advance through collaboration. This pedagogy not
only increases student competency, but educator effectiveness as
well. The key to inclusive pedagogy is understanding the varied
abilities of students and their needs, and collaborating with other
educators to plan and meet these needs.

Both the teacher and the interventionist need to plan together prior to each lesson or unit. Not only can educators learn from PD sessions, but they can learn from one another as well through collaboration.

For example, a novice teacher may know about digital technology, while the veteran teacher may be strong in executing instructional practices, so together they can create a lesson that includes the integration of technology in the classroom, but that is also differentiated for students. Another example would be an interventionist educating a teaching about interventions and supports that may benefit certain students, while the teacher may be able to show the interventionist a different way of approaching the content.

Inclusive pedagogy should be a PD session for educators who work in inclusive classroom settings so that educators understand the importance of collaboration, how to change or add to their current pedagogy, and instructional practices that can be used effectively in inclusive classrooms.

In addition to inclusive pedagogy, educators who work in inclusive classroom settings also need training on collaboration and time management.

Collaboration and Time Management

A PD workshop on collaboration and time management would be helpful to educators who work in inclusive classrooms because Florian (2017) explains that one of the most significant components to inclusive education is collaboration. Also, student achievement is directly related to the collaboration between teachers and interventionists who work in inclusive classroom settings. In order for collaboration to be effective, time management skills need to be a priority as well. If educators are co-teaching, as discussed in the previous chapter, then educators may need to finish a station, or a part of a lesson at a certain time in order to execute the lesson effectively.

Time management is also maximized when educators share the same planning period. Some of the teachers who I co-taught with in the past, and myself, would use our planning periods and lunch times to collaborate. However, not all educators who work with the same students have the same planning period, if they have one at all. Alternative ways to collaborate with other educators, especially in a COVID-19 world, are; email, using a phone, Zoom, Class Dojo, Google Classroom, Apple Classroom, and Microsoft OneNote.

Emails are a way to collaborate with one another because they can be sent, and responded to during a person's convenience. You can also send attachments, videos, and links. Phones are another way to collaborate because educators can call, text, or download certain apps such as: Class Dojo, Google Classroom, or Apple Classroom.

Also, Zoom and Class Dojo are other effective ways to collaborate. When you are having a collaboration session in Zoom, participants are able to take turns sharing their screen, they can record the meeting to refer back to important information, and multiple educators can meet at the same time. However, when using Class Dojo educators can share/create videos as resources for one another, students, and parents. There can also be other posts created that are helpful resources as well, and private messages can be sent to one another. Lastly, there is a Class Story that is available that is similar to social media platforms, but this is private for educators, students, and their parents/guardians.

Google and Apple Classrooms are very similar to one another. Both are online platforms that can be used to communicate and collaborate with other educators, communicate with students and parents, and grade and assign projects and assessments. Links to worksheets and websites, such as ReadWorks, can be embedded in both Google and Apple Classrooms as well. However, Apple Classroom can only be used on an Apple device such as an iPad, which has an enlargement feature for students who have visual impairments.

Microsoft OneNote is another online platform that can be used to collaborate with other educators, and edit documents in real time, without needing to be saved. OneNote can also be used to create lesson plans, or to use for students to create projects, or even to take notes. Multiple Notebooks can be created in OneNote, and within these Notebooks are Sections, and within these Sections are Pages.

In addition to these different platforms that can be used to collaborate, there should also be some time given to anticipated or unanticipated errors during the lesson. Educators should be prepared to anticipate misconceptions, but they should also be prepared with additional resources and materials in case the lesson goes smoother and quicker than expected. It is better to be over-prepared than under-prepared. Time management is also important when differentiating instruction. When instruction is truly being tailored to the needs of students, then there are a lot of entities that need to be considered. In order to keep track of these entities, organization and time management are important.

For example, there are students with a range of abilities in an inclusive classroom setting. With this being said, there are the original lessons and differentiated forms of each lesson, and Response to Intervention also occurs in the classroom. Intervention Specialists have to complete progress reports quarterly, and teachers have to complete report cards quarterly. Also, both parties have to be in attendance at all IEP meetings, and teachers have to be present at 504 Plan meetings. In order to effectively manage all of these entities, time management is key.

Time management is also important for interventionists and teachers for progress monitoring purposes, especially during Response to Intervention (RTI). Time management is also important in order to make sure the correct modifications and accommodations are taking place.

All of these responsibilities and more require excellent time management skills, which is why this should be a required PD session for educators who teach in inclusive classroom settings.

Response to Intervention

Response to Intervention (RTI) is done in the inclusive classroom setting, on a multi-tiered level. Many general education teachers make the mistake of thinking that RTI is the responsibility of the IS, when in fact it is a collaborative effort between both educators. However, most of the heavy lifting is done by general education teachers. RTI is the responsibility of the teacher, to find current reading and math levels of students, to provide differentiated lessons for all, to provide interventions to students, and to monitor their progress. However, when I worked in inclusive classroom settings, as the IS, I would help the teacher provide specific interventions to students who were on Tier 2 or 3 of RTI. I would also provide small group instruction to these students as well as SWD, which included providing interventions when needed.

It is important to have a PD session(s) on RTI so that educators not only understand how to progress monitor and how to work through the different tiers of RTI, but also how to collaborate with one another throughout the process. RTI will be discussed in more detail in the next chapter. If a student reaches Tier 3 interventions and they are still not making adequate progress, then there will be a request for that student to be evaluated to see if they have a disability. If he/she has been diagnosed with having a disability then there are specific modifications and/or accommodations that need to be followed in the student's IEP or 504 Plan.

Modifications and Accommodations

Modifications and accommodations are important for teachers and interventionists to understand, and there should be PD sessions regarding this made available to these educators. These PD sessions would be beneficial for teachers because interventionists are explicitly taught about modifications and accommodations. However, this could also be helpful for interventionists because they need to learn how to collaborate with teachers to make sure modifications and accommodations are being provided to SWD.

Paraprofessionals also need to have an understanding of modifications and accommodations because they are working side-by-side with students all day as well. I have worked in school districts where each student who was diagnosed with a disability had modifications and accommodations present in their IEP or 504 Plan, and I have worked in school districts where each student has accommodations, but not necessarily modifications.

Understanding what modifications and accommodations are, and the difference between them will help maximize effective instruction. Meeting the specific needs of students, and maximizing the effectiveness of instruction will help increase student achievement. Some educators do not understand that modifying a student's work means that there is a change in the content, and the work that a student is supposed to produce.

For example, instead of writing a multi-paragraph response to a writing prompt, a teacher may modify the requirement to a single paragraph response. Additionally, some educators do not understand that accommodating a student means changes that need to occur in the learning environment such as, a student being able to use a multiplication chart to help solve mathematic equations. Understanding modifications and accommodations is also important in understanding the needs of students, and how to differentiate lessons. They serve as a guide on how to help students become successful in inclusive classroom environments. However, regardless of the amount of knowledge that educators possess, it is just as important to have emotional intelligence.

Emotional Intelligence

Daniel Goleman (2015) explains that emotional intelligence is when a person makes decisions based off of their emotions, and the emotions of the people around them. Emotional intelligence is important to have as an educator in general when working with students, collaborating with colleagues, or collaborating with the community. In the classroom an educator must possess emotional intelligence when they are feeling frustrated or upset, or when a student has these emotions, by knowing how to prevent, diffuse, or deescalate a situation. However when working with colleagues, emotional intelligence is also important when collaborating and co-teaching. There needs to be respect for professional opinions, even if there are disagreements, and at times compromises will need to take place amongst educators in order to save our students.

Emotional intelligence is also important to possess when communicating with parents. Parents can become upset for a variety of reasons, but having emotional intelligence allows for the educator to maintain professionalism, understand the concern of the parent, and stay calm to find a solution to the problem. A lack of emotional intelligence will waste time, and inhibit educators from teaching and collaborating effectively. Having emotional intelligence is important when connecting and collaborating with parents, and other members in the community because there are a variety of personalities that will be involved.

Connecting with the Community

Not only are our parents and students a part of the community that we serve in, but there are businesses and nonprofit organizations that are a part of the community that we need to connect and collaborate with as well. Connecting with the community helps educators become more culturally responsive in the community that they serve, and it provides students exposure to opportunities and careers that they may not have been exposed to. Connecting with businesses could enable students to work in the community, train in the community, volunteer in the community, and/or become interested in a career in the future.

Connecting with the community is also important for school districts that lack funds, which causes programs and services to be cut. Nonprofit organizations provide services free of charge, so students are able to have the resources that they need regardless of the lack of funding that their school district may have. Connecting with the community also helps school districts understand what their communities need to thrive.

Putting it All Together

There is a gap in the lack of information that educators receive during teacher preparation programs on how to collaborate and work in inclusive classroom settings. Ongoing PD is needed for educators who work in inclusive classroom environments. While PD sessions should be tailored to the needs of teachers, as much as possible, some PDs should be mandatory for educators who work in inclusive classes. These PDs include: Inclusive Pedagogy, Collaboration and Time Management, Response to Intervention, Modifications and Accommodations, Self-Efficacy and Emotional Intelligence, and Connecting with the Community.

Things to Remember

- The gap in knowledge needs to be filled with PD sessions

- Educators can learn from one another

- Required PDs

  - Inclusive Pedagogy

  - Collaboration and Time Management

  - Response to Intervention

  - Modifications and Accommodations

  - Self-efficacy and Emotional Intelligence

  - Connecting with the Community

General PD for Inclusive Pedagogy

The following PD contains general information for Inclusive Pedagogy, and it may need to be tailored based on staff needs. Additional PDs or work sessions may also be required. Interventionists, teachers, paraprofessionals, and other professionals who work with students in inclusive environments should be present. Each of these professionals can provide insight on diverse entities regarding the same students.

Inclusive Pedagogy

Dr. Donisha N. Bailey

What is Inclusive Pedagogy?

- Student-centered approach

- Contains inclusive practices

- Requires instructional practices to be planned in advance through collaboration

- Key to inclusive pedagogy
  - Collaborating with educators
  - Understanding the various needs of students and how to help them.

Notes

- [ ] _____

- [ ] _____

- [ ] _____

- [ ] _____

- [ ] _____

- [ ] _____

- [ ] _____

- [ ] _____

Why Should we Use Inclusive Pedagogy?

- Enables teachers to meet the needs of ALL students

- Increases student competency

- Increases educator effectiveness

- Enables educators to learn from one another
  - Novice intervention specialist can be skilled in technology
  - Veteran teacher can be skilled in instructional strategies
  - Together they can integrate technology into the classroom through certain instructional strategies

Notes

- [ ] _____

- [ ] _____

- [ ] _____

- [ ] _____

- [ ] _____

- [ ] _____

- [ ] _____

- [ ] _____

Example of Collaboration and Inclusive Pedagogy

- Educators give pre-assessments to students to learn students' varied abilities

- Educators collaborate to assess strengths and weaknesses of students

- Educators anticipate misconceptions

- Educators discuss different instructional strategies and interventions that may be needed

- Educators collaborate to differentiate lessons

Notes

- [ ] _____

- [ ] _____

- [ ] _____

- [ ] _____

- [ ] _____

- [ ] _____

- [ ] _____

- [ ] _____

DO NOT Limit Collaboration

- There should be collaboration amongst many different kinds of educators depending on the needs of students

- Possible professionals who may collaborate in inclusive settings

  - General education teacher
  - Intervention Specialist
  - Paraprofessional
  - Speech and Language Pathologist
  - Occupational Therapist
  - School Psychologist

Notes

- [ ] _____
- [ ] _____
- [ ] _____
- [ ] _____
- [ ] _____
- [ ] _____
- [ ] _____
- [ ] _____

Different Ways to Collaborate

- Not all educational professionals have the same planning periods.

- If you are unable to collaborate in person get creative (especially post COVID-19 world)

- You may collaborate via

  - Email
  - Text messaging
  - Phone call
  - Zoom
  - Class Dojo
  - Google Classroom
  - Apple Classroom
  - Microsoft OneNote

Notes

☐ _____

☐ _____

☐ _____

☐ _____

☐ _____

☐ _____

☐ _____

☐ _____

Notes

- [ ] _____

- [ ] _____

- [ ] _____

- [ ] _____

- [ ] _____

- [ ] _____

- [ ] _____

- [ ] _____

How do you Collaborate?

Notes

- [ ] _____

- [ ] _____

- [ ] _____

- [ ] _____

- [ ] _____

- [ ] _____

- [ ] _____

- [ ] _____

Thoughts on Inclusive Pedagogy

Add your thoughts!

Notes

- [ ] _____

- [ ] _____

- [ ] _____

- [ ] _____

- [ ] _____

- [ ] _____

- [ ] _____

- [ ] _____

General PD for Collaboration & Time Management

The following PD contains general information for Collaboration and Time Management, and it may need to be tailored based on staff needs. Additional PDs or work sessions may also be required. Interventionists, teachers, paraprofessionals, and other professionals who work with students in inclusive environments should be present. Each of these professionals can provide insight on diverse entities regarding the same students.

Collaboration and Time Management

Dr. Donisha N. Bailey

Collaboration

- One of the most significant components of inclusive education

- Student achievement is directly related to the collaboration between educators who work in inclusive settings

- Time management skills are needed to collaborate effectively

Notes

- [ ] _____

- [ ] _____

- [ ] _____

- [ ] _____

- [ ] _____

- [ ] _____

- [ ] _____

- [ ] _____

Time Management

- Time can an be maximized when educators have the same planning periods.

- Time management is important when...

  - Planning, collaborating, and co-teaching
  - Switching classes with other teachers
  - During response to interventions
  - When differentiating lessons
  - Determining possible misconceptions during lesson

- Important when educating or collaborating online

  - Be prepared for technological difficulties
  - Log on early
  - Conduct test runs

Notes

- [ ] _____

- [ ] _____

- [ ] _____

- [ ] _____

- [ ] _____

- [ ] _____

- [ ] _____

- [ ] _____

Ways to Collaborate

- In person during planning periods

- Educators without the same planning periods can...

  - Email
  - Phone (text/call)
  - Zoom
  - Class dojo
  - Google classroom
  - Apple classroom
  - Microsoft OneNote

Notes

- [ ] _____

- [ ] _____

- [ ] _____

- [ ] _____

- [ ] _____

- [ ] _____

- [ ] _____

- [ ] _____

Email and Phone

- Emails

  - Can be sent and responded at convenience
  - Can send attachments, video, etc.

- Phone

  - Call
  - Text
  - Can download Class Dojo app, Google Classroom app, Apple Classroom app

Notes

- [ ] _____

- [ ] _____

- [ ] _____

- [ ] _____

- [ ] _____

- [ ] _____

- [ ] _____

- [ ] _____

Zoom and Class Dojo

- Zoom

  - Share screen
  - Record meeting
  - Meet with multiple educational professionals at once

- Class dojo

  - Share/create videos
  - Posts (resources, class projects, etc.)
  - Messages
  - Class story (similar to social media platforms, but private for teachers, students, and their parents/ guardians)

Notes

- [ ] _____

- [ ] _____

- [ ] _____

- [ ] _____

- [ ] _____

- [ ] _____

- [ ] _____

- [ ] _____

Google & Apple Classroom

- Google classroom

  - Online platform to collaborate
  - Able to communicate with students
  - Able to assign, grade, and/or embed...
    - Assignments
    - Projects
    - Assessments
    - Links to worksheets
    - Links to websites (i.e. ReadWorks)

- Apple classroom

  - Similar to google classroom, but w/ iPad only
  - Contains feature that enlarges texts for students with visual impairments

Notes

- [ ] _____

- [ ] _____

- [ ] _____

- [ ] _____

- [ ] _____

- [ ] _____

- [ ] _____

- [ ] _____

Microsoft OneNote

- Online platform

- Able to be edited in real time by all educators

- Able to create lesson plans

- Able to use for students to create projects

- Able to create multiple notebooks

- Sections within notebooks

- Pages within sections

Notes

- [ ] _____

- [ ] _____

- [ ] _____

- [ ] _____

- [ ] _____

- [ ] _____

- [ ] _____

- [ ] _____

Which Platforms Have You Used to Collaborate and/or Educate?

Add your thoughts!

Notes

- [ ] _____
- [ ] _____
- [ ] _____
- [ ] _____
- [ ] _____
- [ ] _____
- [ ] _____
- [ ] _____

Chapter 3

Response to Intervention and Progress Monitoring

"Just because we have the best hammer does not mean that every problem is a nail."

-President Barack Obama

R esponse to Intervention (RTI) is multi-tiered, and it provides targeted instruction to students who are struggling in the classroom. A major component to RTI is progress monitoring. If educators do not understand how to respond to intervention, or how to monitor progress, then they cannot identify and help students who are performing below grade level. If educators are unable to identify students who are struggling then they cannot save our students. If educators are able to identify the struggling students, but they do not know how to conduct RTI practices then they are unable to save our students.

Response to Intervention

According to the RTI Action Network, there are 3 Tiers to

RTI, Tiers 1, 2, and 3. During Tier 1 high-quality instruction is supposed to be provided to all students, and through state and district assessments teachers identify students who are struggling in inclusive classroom settings. Students who are struggling are given additional support such as small group instruction, or other supplemental instruction. This tier generally does not exceed 8 weeks. During this time these students' progress is monitored, using curriculum based assessments, or other screening systems that are validated. If students are improving then they return to the regular classroom program, but if they are not showing adequate progress then these students move to Tier 2 instruction.

Tier 2 of RTI consists of targeted interventions that are more intense in order to further meet the needs of struggling students. This tier may take more time than Tier 1, but generally does not last longer than a quarter, or 9 weeks. During this tier, as the interventionist, I pull students for small group instruction with SWD so that they are provided with more intense intervention. While this is not a requirement, ultimately as educators we need to do what is best for all students. Teachers who are not a part of a co-teaching setting with an IS provide small group instruction to Tier 2 students, that is more focused and intense than Tier 1. However, even without a co-teacher it is wise to consult an interventionist because they specialize in providing interventions to students who are performing below grade level.

During Tier 3 of RTI students' deficits are targeted even more and instruction is more individualized and intense than Tiers 1 and 2. Not only are interventionists who are working in inclusive classroom settings working in small groups with Tier 3 students, but students may also be provided with additional services such as tutoring. Students who do not show adequate progress during this tier are recommended for testing to see if they are diagnosed with a disability, and receive services under the Individuals with Disabilities Education Improvement Act of 2004 (IDEA 2004).

Progress Monitoring

All of the data that was collected from Tiers 1, 2, and 3 will play a role, in addition to testing, in the determination of whether or not a student may begin receiving special education services. This is why progress monitoring is the main component of RTI. Which leads to the importance of educators who work in inclusive classroom settings being professionally developed on RTI, and how to collaborate with one another effectively to provide the best instruction for all students. Many times teachers see a test score and receive classwork, and they can identify right away students who are struggling. However, all students who struggle in the beginning of a school year are not in need of special education services. That is why RTI is an essential part of inclusive classroom settings. I have seen teachers try to cut corners and speed up the process of testing a student to see if he/she qualifies for services, I have even wanted to at times because I wanted students to get the support they needed. However, I was giving them the support that they needed during RTI anyway, so they were being serviced, just not officially. Also, trying to speed up the RTI process will cause for a lack of data on the progress of the student. Some teachers are also not progress monitoring often enough, if at all. This could be for many reasons, including the lack of a complete understanding of the RTI process. This is where PD sessions on RTI are effective.

Again, I would not limit these PDs to teachers and interventionists, I would open it up to paraprofessionals as well, but each session would be specific to the needs of the educators, after a general session has been given. It is important for educators who work in inclusive settings in any capacity to understand RTI, how to implement RTI, and how to progress monitor. Once a student has been diagnosed with a disability then it is essential to understand the students IEP or 504 Plan, and how to implement modifications and/or accommodations into their learning.

Putting it All Together

Response to Intervention (RTI) is a multi-tiered approach to help struggling students by putting interventions in place, and to reveal students who may need to be tested to see if they qualify to receive special education services. A large part of RTI is progress monitoring. Therefore, it is essential for administrators to provide educators, who work in inclusive classrooms, with PD sessions that help them understand RTI and progress monitoring.

Things to Remember

- RTI includes Tiers 1, 2, 3

- Teachers and interventionists should collaborate to find interventions specific to the needs of students who are working through RTI tiers.

- All educators who work in inclusive settings need PD sessions on RTI and progress monitoring.

- Make sure enough data is collected, and student progress is monitored regularly.

- Not all students who go through RTI are diagnosed with a disability.

- Students who are diagnosed with a disability will receive an IEP or 504 Plan.

General PD for RTI

The following PD contains general information for RTI, and it may need to be tailored based on staff needs. Additional PDs or work sessions may also be required. Educators should bring student work samples, and discuss different ways to respond to intervention. Interventionists, teachers, and paraprofessionals should be present. Each of these professionals can provide insight on diverse entities regarding the same students.

Response to Intervention (RTI)

Dr. Donisha N. Bailey

What is Response to Intervention?

- RTI is...
  - Multi-tiered
  - Provides instruction to struggling students

- Progress monitoring is a major component

- Important to understand to identify struggling students

Notes

- [ ] _____

- [ ] _____

- [ ] _____

- [ ] _____

- [ ] _____

- [ ] _____

- [ ] _____

- [ ] _____

Tier 1

- High-quality instruction for all students

- Identification of struggling students via...

  - District assessments
  - Curriculum-based assessments
  - State assessments

- Small group or supplemental instruction

- Progress monitoring usually does not exceed 8 weeks.

- Students who do not improve move to tier 2

Notes

- [ ] _____
- [ ] _____
- [ ] _____
- [ ] _____
- [ ] _____
- [ ] _____
- [ ] _____
- [ ] _____

Tier 2

- Targeted, more focused and intense instruction

  - General education teacher
  - Intervention specialist

- Intervention specialist may provide small group instruction with specific interventions

- Progress monitoring generally not longer than a quarter (9 weeks)

- Students who do not improve move to tier 3

Notes

- [ ] _____
- [ ] _____
- [ ] _____
- [ ] _____
- [ ] _____
- [ ] _____
- [ ] _____
- [ ] _____

Tier 3

- Student deficits are targeted even more

- More intense interventions are provided by...
  - Intervention specialists
  - Tutors
  - Teachers (small groups within classroom)

- Progress monitoring generally takes about 8 weeks

- Students who do not improve are recommended that they are tested to see if they qualify for special education services.

Notes

- [ ] _____

- [ ] _____

- [ ] _____

- [ ] _____

- [ ] _____

- [ ] _____

- [ ] _____

- [ ] _____

Progress Monitoring

- Data and information from all 3 tiers

  - Tier 1- at least 8 weeks
  - Tier 2- at least 9 weeks
  - Tier 3- at least 8 weeks

- Combination of data from progress monitoring and testing

- Progress monitor often (daily, weekly,)

  - Daily can be informal w/ quick checks or formal w/ exit slips
  - Weekly via work samples and/or quizzes

- Work samples needed for each week

Notes

- [ ] _____

- [ ] _____

- [ ] _____

- [ ] _____

- [ ] _____

- [ ] _____

- [ ] _____

- [ ] _____

Tips on Progress Monitoring

- Collaborate with other educational professionals on a regular basis to analyze deficits

  - Teacher and interventionist collaborate
  - Teacher and interventionist, collaborate with paraprofessional

- Keep well documented records

  - Work samples
  - Data from assessments
  - Anecdotal records

- DO NOT CUT CORNERS

  - A lack of data will lead to the need for more data
  - Make sure you can show data over a progression of many weeks as described throughout the multi-tiered process

Notes

- [ ] _____
- [ ] _____
- [ ] _____
- [ ] _____
- [ ] _____
- [ ] _____
- [ ] _____
- [ ] _____

Collaborative Efforts

- Requires teacher to identify struggling students and collaborate with interventionist

- Interventionist will observe and provide possible interventions for teacher to use

- Teachers should heed these suggestions

- Paraprofessionals should not be left out

- Parents should not be left out

Notes

- [ ] _____

- [ ] _____

- [ ] _____

- [ ] _____

- [ ] _____

- [ ] _____

- [ ] _____

- [ ] _____

Tips on Collaborative Efforts

- Respect one another's expertise

- Learn from one another

- Maintain emotional intelligence

- Do not be afraid to research interventions or research-based instructional strategies

- WE DO NOT KNOW IT ALL, SUPPORT ONE ANOTHER, ALWAYS BE WILLING TO LEARN

Notes

- [ ] _____
- [ ] _____
- [ ] _____
- [ ] _____
- [ ] _____
- [ ] _____
- [ ] _____
- [ ] _____

Students who go through RTI Process

- Not all students who go through RTI are diagnosed with disability

- Some students improve throughout RTI

- Some students will be diagnosed with a disability and qualify for Individualized Education Program (IEP)

- Some students will be diagnosed with a disability, but they will qualify for a 504 Plan instead of IEP

Notes

- [ ] _____

- [ ] _____

- [ ] _____

- [ ] _____

- [ ] _____

- [ ] _____

- [ ] _____

- [ ] _____

Chapter 4

Modifications and Accommodations

"The important thing about a problem is not its solution, but the strength we gain in finding the solution ."

-Seneca the Younger

There is a wide-range of abilities in inclusion classroom settings amongst students who have and who do not have disabilities. According to The Ohio Department of Education, amongst the special education population 75% of students do not have general cognitive performance deficits as a feature of their disability. This means the vast majority of students are being educated in inclusive classroom settings. Students' needs vary considerably because their abilities vary. The majority of students with disabilities are able to meet the same high achievement standards as students without disabilities when provided with effective instruction, accommodations and modifications.

Legally speaking, accommodations and modifications are required for SWD to successfully access the general curriculum, and to determine if students are making progress in meeting their goals and objectives. The determination of accommodations and modifications needed for students to access the general education curriculum is based on the academic content standards and the student's needs.

Modifications

Modifications are changes in the content that students are supposed to master. An example of this would be modifying expectations for a writing assignment from three paragraphs to one paragraph, or completing half of a test, or an assignment. I have walked into many inclusive classroom settings as an observer, an Intervention Specialist, and a Dean of Students, and I have witnessed a lack of modifications, and a lack of differentiation in general, which has at times led to teacher frustration, and poor classroom management. The student's work was not being modified, and some of the teachers that I observed had no idea how to help these students.

I remember facilitating a PD session about modifications and accommodations while working at a charter school before I became a licensed interventionist. The session was an hour long, and at the end of the session the staff members looked puzzled, and they had so many unanswered questions. There was no follow-up training, or another training that came close to this PD session. The interventionists were trying to intervene, and help with the explanation of the differences between modifications and accommodations, but the vast majority of the staff was not comfortable with understanding the difference between them, or each entity individually for that matter.

At the end of the meeting the Principal made it clear that all SWD should have their work modified by 50%. She explained that the students would be responsible for completing half of their work, and the other half they would automatically receive credit for.

For example, if there was a ten question quiz, the student would have to complete five questions, and if they completed all five questions correctly they would have 100%, but if they missed two problems they would have a 70% (7/10) instead of a 60% (3/5). While I appreciate the Principal's attempt to be an advocate for SWD in her own way, this modification may not have been needed for students who were performing higher than others, or it may not have been enough for students who had needs that were more severe.

Modifications should be specific to students' educational needs.

This is a part of how lessons are differentiated by educators. Understanding both modifications and accommodations will be a guide for educators to tailor lessons to students based on their needs.

Accommodations

The term accommodation refers to the change(s) to the learning environment including the equipment that is available, and how assessments/assignments are completed. Some examples of accommodations for a student would be extended time to take assessments, small group testing, and frequent breaks. Accommodations are important because some students only need extra time, not necessarily a modified curriculum, to successfully complete assignments.

As an interventionist, I have worked in inclusive classroom settings where I pushed into the classroom, and I took students to the resource room to give them as much time as they needed to complete assignments or assessments. I have also worked in inclusive settings where teachers have gotten upset with special needs students, and they start rushing students to complete their work, or the teacher appears to be irritated because directions have to be given repeatedly.

Administrative Responsibilities

Educators have a legal obligation to follow student's IEPs and 504 Plans, and this includes following the accommodations and/or modifications that are in these documents. There needs to be an understanding of how accommodations are changes that need to be made so that SWD can successfully access the general education curriculum in inclusive classes. There also needs to be an understanding of how modifications are not commonly seen in inclusive classrooms because many students do not require them.

It is important for teachers to be familiar with all aspects of students' IEPs and 504 plans because there may not always be an interventionist in the room. However, teachers and interventionists are not the only educators who work with students directly in the inclusive classroom setting. Paraprofessionals are also responsible for knowing and understanding the legal documents that pertain to the student's education who they work with.

Being that paraprofessionals are not licensed educators, there is a gap in teacher education programs pertaining to inclusive education and collaboration for novice educators, and there were no inclusion settings when most veteran teachers were being educated, professional development is the key to helping all of these educators develop and grow. A major part of administrative responsibility is to make sure that students have highly qualified professionals in front of them to enhance their achievement. In addition to teacher preparation programs, or the lack thereof, because qualifications differ from paraprofessionals to teachers, to interventionists, administrators need to have PD sessions tailored to all educators, as much as possible, who work in inclusive classroom environments.

While collaboration and training teachers is a part of promoting school inclusion, the PD sessions that are needed should not be limited to certain educators, and the sessions should not be limited to information about special education, working in inclusive classes, or how to collaborate with other educators. PD sessions should also include sessions such as emotional intelligence and connecting with the community, as well as any other personalized professional development sessions that may be needed.

Putting it All Together

Differentiating lessons for students should be based on their abilities, and the modifications and/or accommodations that are in their IEP or 504 Plan. Also, IEPs and 504 Plans are legal documents that need to be understood by all educators who work in inclusive classroom settings with students. It is the responsibility of administration to put the proper PD sessions in place to develop teachers, interventionists, and paraprofessionals who all work in inclusive classroom environments.

Things to Remember

- Modifications and accommodations are important to tailor lessons to students' needs so that they can be successful in the classroom.

- Modification- Change in the content and the expectation of student work production.

- Accommodation- Changes how students are learning (such as using a multiplication chart to aide in multi-step multiplication equations).

- Some students may not need modifications to the content, only an accommodation such as extended time.

- Administrators are responsible for providing adequate PD sessions so that staff members are informed, so that they are at their best when working in inclusive classroom settings.

- Administrators should include paraprofessionals in PD sessions involving inclusion education.

- PD sessions should not be limited to information about special education, collaboration, and inclusive education, but also emotional intelligence, and how to connect and collaborate with the community.

General PD for Modifications & Accommodations

The following PD is general information for modifications and accommodations, and it may need to be tailored based on staff needs. Additional PDs or work sessions may also be required. Educators should bring student work samples, and discuss different ways to modify work and make accommodations for students. Interventionists, teachers, and paraprofessionals should be present. Each of these professionals can provide insight on diverse entities regarding the same students.

Modifications and Accommodations

Dr. Donisha N. Bailey

Modifications

- A modification is a change in the content that students are required to master.

- Examples

  - Original assignment: produce 3 paragraph essay
  - Modified assignment: produce 1 paragraph
  - Modify the curriculum by 50%
  - The amount of homework can be modified

- The IEP team determines modifications needed for specific students, if at all, in IEP

- The 504 evaluation team determines modifications needed for specific students, if at all, in 504 Plan.

Notes

- [ ] _____

- [ ] _____

- [ ] _____

- [ ] _____

- [ ] _____

- [ ] _____

- [ ] _____

- [ ] _____

Where Can I Locate Modifications?

- IEP: located in Section 7- Description of Specially Designed Services

- IEP: provides information on the specific modification(s), and the dates it will be effective.

- 504 Plan: located in Section 2- Accommodations/ Modifications/ Intervention/Services/Aids

- 504 Plan: provides information on the substantial limitation, the actual modification, the person responsible, the location, and the start date.

Notes

- [ ] _____
- [ ] _____
- [ ] _____
- [ ] _____
- [ ] _____
- [ ] _____
- [ ] _____
- [ ] _____

Let's Discuss Modifications

- Educators should bring work samples to show how they modified students' work.

- Educators should use this opportunity to discuss specific examples of how students' work was modified.

- This is an opportunity for collaboration

- Referring back to the IEP or 504 Plan on a regular basis is encouraged.

- ALL educators who are working with these students should be well versed in the contents of both IEPs and 504 Plans

Notes

- [ ] _____
- [ ] _____
- [ ] _____
- [ ] _____
- [ ] _____
- [ ] _____
- [ ] _____
- [ ] _____

Accommodations

- Accommodations are changes to the learning environment including the equipment that is available, and how assessments/ assignments are completed.

- Examples of Accommodations

  - Preferential seating
  - Small group testing
  - Use of Multiplication Charts for math
  - Use of graphic organizers for writing

- The IEP team determines accommodations that are needed for specific students in IEP

- The 504 evaluation team determines accommodations needed for specific students in 504 Plan.

Notes

- [ ] _____

- [ ] _____

- [ ] _____

- [ ] _____

- [ ] _____

- [ ] _____

- [ ] _____

- [ ] _____

Where do I Locate Accommodations?

- IEP:

  - Section 7- Description of Specially Designed Services
  - Section 12- Statewide and District Testing

- IEP: provides information on the specific accommodations, and the dates it will be effective.

- 504 Plan:

  - Section 2- Accommodations/Modifications/Intervention/ Services/Aids
  - Section 3- Statewide/District Testing

- 504 Plan: provides info on the substantial limitation, actual accommodations, person responsible, location, and start date.

Notes

- [ ] _____
- [ ] _____
- [ ] _____
- [ ] _____
- [ ] _____
- [ ] _____
- [ ] _____
- [ ] _____

Let's Discuss Accommodations

- Educators should bring work samples or information to show how they accommodate students.

- This is an opportunity for collaboration

- Referring back to the IEP or 504 Plan on a regular basis is encouraged.

- ALL educators who are working with these students should be well versed in the contents of both IEPs and 504 Plans

Notes

- ☐ _____

- ☐ _____

- ☐ _____

- ☐ _____

- ☐ _____

- ☐ _____

- ☐ _____

- ☐ _____

Differentiation

- Differentiation is tailoring instruction so that specific needs of students are met.

- Differentiation is done when modifying students' work.

- Differentiation is done when accommodating students.

- Modifications and/or accommodations are the guide on how to differentiate lessons for students.

- Additional measures can be taken that are not in IEP and/or 504 plan such as creating opportunities for peer learning, or using sentence starters to help with writing.

Notes

- [ ] _____

- [ ] _____

- [ ] _____

- [ ] _____

- [ ] _____

- [ ] _____

- [ ] _____

- [ ] _____

Chapter 5

Self-Efficacy and Emotional Intelligence

"If you're emotional abilities are not in hand, if you don't have self-awareness, if you are not able to manage your distressing emotions, if you can't have empathy and have effective relationships, then no matter how smart you are, you are not going to get very far."

-Daniel Goleman

It is important that a high quality education is provided to all students who learn in inclusive classroom environments. In order to do this, educators need to be properly trained, they need to have a high sense of self-efficacy, and they need to be emotionally intelligent. Educators also need to feel supported by administration, and prepared in order to work effectively in inclusive classes, and to save our students.

Self-Efficacy

Self-efficacy is how people perceive their abilities to achieve goals (Emmons & Zager, 2017; Ruppar et al., 2016). Teachers' attitudes towards inclusive education are related to their sense of self-efficacy, and this can directly affect how inclusive practices are executed (Yada, Savolainen, 2017). If teachers are resistant to being developed professionally this could lead to low self-efficacy, and a lack of instructional growth. Teacher self-efficacy can also be affected when teachers do not feel properly trained to do their jobs effectively. Administrative support and collaboration can lead to positive teacher attitudes regarding inclusive education and training, which leads to equal educational opportunities for all students. Teachers who have positive attitudes towards inclusive education tend to be more willing to attend workshops or sessions that they can learn from, and that will make them a better educator overall.

Another entity that adds to teachers positive attitudes towards inclusive education and training is professional development. According to Driver & Murphy (2018), more and more novice teachers are reporting that they are not fully equipped with the knowledge and tools that they need to work in inclusive classroom settings. If teachers feel secure in their abilities to teach they have a high sense of self-efficacy; they can maximize their instruction in inclusive settings; and they can provide a high quality education to all students.

Educators self-efficacy can also affect how they collaborate.

The more educators are involved in inclusive practices, such as collaboration, the more positive their attitudes are towards training and learning not only from PD sessions, but from their colleagues as well. However, a part of being able to collaborate effectively is respecting individual professional opinions and experiences, and being emotionally intelligent.

Emotional Intelligence

According to Daniel Goleman (2015), emotional intelligence is the ability of people being able to recognize their emotions and the emotions of others, and the ability to use emotional information to guide their behavior and thinking. The fundamentals of emotional intelligence are self-awareness, self-management, social awareness, and the ability to manage relationships. Emotional intelligence includes being able to listen and cooperate with others, that is why it is important to have emotional intelligence when collaborating with other educators, so that everyone's thoughts and ideas are heard and respected, in an effort to make the best decisions for students to succeed.

Similarly, Doug Lemov (2015) explains that emotional consistency is the lessening of the intensity of strong emotions, including disappointment and frustrations. Emotional consistency is important whether educators are in the classroom with students, or outside of the classroom collaborating with other educators. How people feel and behave makes a difference in how they collaborate (Kouzes & Posner, 2017).

Authenticity

Collaboration and ongoing PD are important, but we must never forget to be authentic above all. Educators should not be afraid to let their personality shine through! Children love excitement and connections with their work through joy and color, and they can sense when educators are not being authentic or genuine. As educators we must never let ourselves get so bogged down with collaborating, organizing, and learning that we forget to connect with our students on a human level.

Connecting with students means knowing their interests, which can help when you are differentiating a lesson, or finding reading materials based on students' reading levels. If you know that a student is interested in sports, or even a specific genre of reading such as non-fiction, this is useful information when planning and collaborating in order to make the learning fun for that particular student. Building rapport with students is important because with rapport comes trust, and when students are interested and they trust their teachers, they are more open and willing to learn. However, our students are part of a community, and it is also important to connect with the community and to build a rapport and trust as well.

Putting it all together

Educators need to be confident, or have a high sense of self-efficacy, so that they can maximize their instructional practices in the classroom. Teachers' attitudes towards inclusive education and professional development can directly affect their ability to provide high quality instruction to students. Also, it is important to have emotional intelligence regardless of what role you are serving in education. A part of collaborating successfully is having emotional intelligence. Emotional intelligence is needed when dealing with students, parents, and other educators. Lastly, it is important to be yourself and build rapport and trust with students and the rest of the community.

Things to Remember

- Self-efficacy is how people perceive their own abilities.

- High self-efficacy leads to high quality instruction

- Emotional Intelligence is the ability to understand your emotions and the people around you, and to make decisions based on that information.

- Emotional consistency is the lessening of strong intense emotions

- Be authentic in collaboration and in the classroom.

- Make learning fun, and let your personality shine through!

General PD for Self-efficacy & Emotional Intelligence

The following PD contains general information for self-efficacy and emotional intelligence, and it may need to be tailored based on staff needs. Additional PDs or work sessions may also be required. Interventionists, teachers, and paraprofessionals should be present. Each of these professionals can provide insight on diverse entities regarding the same students, and they all need a high-sense of self-efficacy and to be emotionally intelligent when educating students, and when collaborating with parents and other educators.

Self-Efficacy and Emotional Intelligence

Dr. Donisha N. Bailey

What is Self-Efficacy

- Self-efficacy is how people perceive their abilities to achieve goals.

- Teachers' attitudes towards inclusive education are related to self-efficacy.

- Teachers' self-efficacy can directly affect how inclusive practices are executed.

- Positive attitudes = High sense of self-efficacy = effective instruction = student achievement

- Negative attitudes = Low sense of self-efficacy = ineffective instruction = lack of student achievement

Notes

- [ ] _____

- [ ] _____

- [ ] _____

- [ ] _____

- [ ] _____

- [ ] _____

- [ ] _____

- [ ] _____

How to Improve your own Self-Efficacy

- Have a positive attitude towards...

  - Inclusive education
  - Professions development
  - Collaboration

- Be willing to learn via

  - PD sessions
  - Work sessions
  - Other colleagues

- Collaborate with

  - Other educational professional who work with students in inclusive environments
  - This may include support services such as SLP and OT.

Notes

- [ ] _____

- [ ] _____

- [ ] _____

- [ ] _____

- [ ] _____

- [ ] _____

- [ ] _____

- [ ] _____

What is Emotional Intelligence (EI)?

- Emotional intelligence is the ability of people being able to recognize their emotions and the emotions of others, and the ability to use this information to guide their behavior and thinking.

- Fundamentals of EI include...
  - Self-awareness
  - Self-management
  - Social-awareness
  - Ability to manage relationships

Notes

- [ ] _____

- [ ] _____

- [ ] _____

- [ ] _____

- [ ] _____

- [ ] _____

- [ ] _____

- [ ] _____

How to Improve Emotional Intelligence

- Be willing to

  - Listen
  - Cooperate
  - Compromise
  - Empathetic

- When collaborating

  - Respect others' professional input
  - Be open to new ideas
  - Always do what is best for the student (not your comfort)

Notes

- [ ] _____

- [ ] _____

- [ ] _____

- [ ] _____

- [ ] _____

- [ ] _____

- [ ] _____

- [ ] _____

What is Emotional Consistency?

- Emotional consistency is the lessening of the intensity of strong emotions, including disappointment and frustrations.

- Emotional consistency is important...

  - Inside of the classroom with students
  - Inside of the classroom with other educators
  - Outside of the classroom during collaboration

Notes

- [ ] _____
- [ ] _____
- [ ] _____
- [ ] _____
- [ ] _____
- [ ] _____
- [ ] _____
- [ ] _____

How to Improve Emotional Consistency

- Be empathetic to students, YOU DO NOT KNOW THE WHOLE STORY (outside of school)

- How people feel and behave makes a difference in how they collaborate

- Maintaining emotional consistency means you are emotionally intelligent on a regular basis

- Be authentic and collaborate in a way to make learning fun.

- Let your personality shine through! (don't be a robot)

Notes

- [ ] _____

- [ ] _____

- [ ] _____

- [ ] _____

- [ ] _____

- [ ] _____

- [ ] _____

- [ ] _____

Notes

- [ ] _____

- [ ] _____

- [ ] _____

- [ ] _____

- [ ] _____

- [ ] _____

- [ ] _____

- [ ] _____

Chapter 6

Connecting with the Community

"Education is for improving the lives of others and for leaving your community and world better than you found it."

-Marian Wright Edelman

Collaboration is not only important in the inclusive classroom setting, but in the community as well. Connecting with the community is another way to save our students. There are many diverse ways for educators to connect with the community. The community members that educators connect with first are students and their parents. Educators are with their students each day, and they need to connect with them inside of the classroom. There should be constant communication with student's families whether it is through a weekly newsletter, a daily behavior log, or a bi-weekly check-in.

There should also be connections made to businesses and nonprofit organizations in the community to expose our children to different resources and careers, so that they understand that with hard work and dedication they have many opportunities, some in which they have never imagined.

Connecting with Students and Families

Some of the ways that I've connected with students would be through interest surveys at the beginning of the school year. The surveys would include information such as their favorite color, food, book, subject, their least favorite subject, and more. I would also have conversations with students during various opportunities in class. I built trust and rapport with students by giving immediate feedback, while I circulated the classroom. During independent learning, during small group instruction, or during my anticipatory set, I made sure to support their learning. Whenever there was an opportunity for me to connect with my students I did. I always listened to their thoughts, feelings, and thinking process.

I also connected with parents through weekly newsletters, daily behavior logs, Class Dojo, and phone calls, emails, and text messages. However, implementing a parent university or a program similar would encourage parents to be more involved, and it would educate them on entities such as math strategies, so that they can help their children with their homework, and studying for tests. Over the last three years many parents have explained that they were unable to help their children with math equations because they did not understand the new strategies that we were teaching students. Also, having events like Muffins for Moms or Donuts for Dads, helps connect schools with the community as well. Providing parents with opportunities to read to a classroom is another way to get parents, and the rest of the community involved in the schools. Also, chaperoning on field trips, or speaking for career day are opportunities to include parents, and other members in the community, and it is another way to connect with parents.

Parents know their children also, and collaboration amongst parents and educators can help students at home, and it can help their performance in the classroom. If there is consistency between what is going on at home and in school, then the student will improve academically, and behaviorally if that is what is needed. For example, if a parent and teacher collaborate and find that routines are what is best for the student, then a teacher can make a daily, weekly, or monthly schedule for the student so that is a part of his/her routine.

Also, if a student starts his/her day in a negative way then that can be communicated to the teacher so that he/she is aware of the emotional state of the student, and can use that information to prevent escalated behavior, in an effort to be proactive instead of reactive.

Saving our students is about presently saving the community, and preparing students so that they can save their communities in the future. One of the ways that we can prepare students to save the community in the future is by doing our part to help make them prominent members of society. One way to do this is by connecting and collaborating with businesses.

Connecting with Businesses

Collaborating and connecting with businesses in the community are important for multiple reasons. First, it is important to expose students to different career opportunities that they may not be exposed to on a regular basis. Students may know that there are policemen in the community, but they may not understand the levels and ranks of police officers until they meet them, and learn more about the different careers within law enforcement. Especially with the negative connotations that are currently attached to the law enforcement field today. Students may be motivated to make a change in law enforcement, and simultaneously it may become a career they are interested in.

Another reason why it is important to give students experiences with different kinds of careers is to help them spark an interest in a career that they may be interested in, and that they may want to learn more about. Exposure and experience are important when collaborating with businesses in the community because students can obtain mentors, or professionals can visit schools for more than just career day, but to help with a project.

For example, an engineer could work with a group of students to build something for their school, or a banker may spark a financial interest in a student. Other students may be more intrigued by being a type of scientist, such as a food scientist. However, these students will never know all of the careers and fields that they may be interested in unless they are exposed to them. Connecting with businesses and nonprofit organizations are also important because it provides a better context for real world learning through experiences, and they are also provided with access to additional resources.

Also, connecting with nonprofit organizations is just as important, if not more important, than connecting with businesses, especially nonprofits that work with academics, social emotional learning, and mentoring. Nonprofit organizations that work specifically with students to improve their skills are valuable because many tutoring programs have either been cut due to a lack of funding, or they never existed.

Connecting with Nonprofit Organizations

It is important to connect with nonprofit organizations in the community because they will provide additional services for students that may not currently be provided in their district. For example, I worked for a school that provided tutoring services for students throughout the week, as well as Saturday school, but when funding was cut tutoring was one of the first entities to be cut. The same issue occurred when I worked at a different school.

As a result, I created a nonprofit organization to help improve literacy through writing, speaking and listening skills, called The Literacy Club with Dr. Bailey (T.L.C. with Dr. B.). Just because funding is gone, does not mean additional services, such as additional literacy support, are no longer needed. It means districts need to take this opportunity to connect with nonprofit organizations in the community to continue providing resources for students.

Some additional nonprofit organizations may include mentoring programs or programs that focus on character education and other social/emotional aspects. Not all students struggle academically, some students have behaviors that impede their learning, so social/emotional programs would be beneficial in these cases. Students would be able to role-play, or respond to a scenario in a responsible manner.

There are some nonprofit organizations that cater specifically to the needs of SWD, they may help students find jobs, get into a college, or understand the interview process. Most of these services and resources are found by the IS during transition years beginning at age 14. There are many nonprofit organizations that can be used to benefit students academically, socially, emotionally, and behaviorally throughout the school year and over the summer.

However, we have to make these services available to our students. If these services and resources are available to students, and they do not know where to find them, or how to access them, then they will not benefit from them. Also, some nonprofit organizations tend to connect and work with other nonprofit organizations, which can lead to a plethora of resources, activities, lessons, and events that are made available to students.

Putting it all Together

Collaborating with the community is important to provide additional resources to students to help them succeed. Collaboration and connections with students and their families is important to build rapport and trust. Collaborating with businesses gives students exposure to careers and experiences that they generally may not have had. Collaborating with nonprofit organizations are important because they can provide additional services that may have been cut by funding, or that were never available in the first place. They can also provide networking opportunities to work with other nonprofit organizations.

The categories and complexity of the community varies from district to district and community to community (Vollmer, 2010). It is important to carefully break down the available resources in the community so that students have access to a variety of resources to help them become successful. Also, when educators collaborate amongst one another, and then they collaborate with outside sources it makes the connection even more powerful because different people bring different strengths to a team. Within this team people also have different connections that expand the networking opportunities that students will have access to.

Saving our students entails an ongoing effort to make sure that educators are at their best, so that they can give all students their best. It is an ongoing effort of the professional development of educators, especially in the categories of inclusive pedagogy, collaboration between professionals, time management, responding to interventions, progress monitoring, accommodating students and modifying student work, self-efficacy, and emotional intelligence. It is also an ongoing effort to connect and collaborate with the community.

Things to Remember

- Collaborating with the community benefits students.

- Collaboration and connections should also take place with:

    ○ Students and families

    ○ Businesses

    ○ Nonprofit organizations

- Collaborating with the community gives students exposure and experience.

- Saving our students is not one entity, but a collaboration of many entities, and diverse educators who will increase student success and achievement inside and outside of the classroom.

General PD for Connecting with Communities

The following PD contains general information about connecting with different parts of the community. Additional PDs or work sessions may also be required. Interventionists, teachers, and paraprofessionals should be present. Each of these professionals can provide insight on diverse entities regarding the same students.

Connecting with the Community

Dr. Donisha N. Bailey

Connection and Collaboration

- Collaborating with the community is important.

- Many diverse ways to connect with community...

  - Build rapport with students
  - Collaborate with parents/families
  - Connect with businesses
  - Connect with nonprofit organizations

Notes

- [ ] _____

- [ ] _____

- [ ] _____

- [ ] _____

- [ ] _____

- [ ] _____

- [ ] _____

- [ ] _____

Connecting with Students and Families

- These are the first members of the community that we build rapport, connect, and collaborate with.

- Ways to connect with students
  - Learn about their culture
  - Learn about their interests
  - Listen to them
  - Provide resources that they are interested in to make learning fun

- Ways to connect with families
  - Daily behavior log
  - Weekly newsletter
  - Bi-weekly check-ins
  - Make positive phone calls
  - Class Dojo
  - Parent university

Notes

- [ ] _____

- [ ] _____

- [ ] _____

- [ ] _____

- [ ] _____

- [ ] _____

- [ ] _____

- [ ] _____

Connecting with Businesses

- Students receive exposure to potential careers that they may be interested in.

- Students can gain experiences with different kinds of careers to help them spark an interest in a career.

- Exposure and experience are important because students can obtain mentors, or professionals can participate in more than just career day, possibly helping with a project.

Notes

- [ ] _____
- [ ] _____
- [ ] _____
- [ ] _____
- [ ] _____
- [ ] _____
- [ ] _____
- [ ] _____

Connecting with Non-Profit Organizations

- Supplemental services can be provided to students

- School district budgets are cut so are services such as tutoring

- Students still need additional support

- Seek out non-profit organizations to continue supplemental services.

- Some nonprofits provide
  - Educational services
  - Socio-emotional services
  - Behavioral services

Notes

- [ ] _____
- [ ] _____
- [ ] _____
- [ ] _____
- [ ] _____
- [ ] _____
- [ ] _____
- [ ] _____

Notes

- [ ] _____

- [ ] _____

- [ ] _____

- [ ] _____

- [ ] _____

- [ ] _____

- [ ] _____

- [ ] _____

Notes

- [ ] _____
- [ ] _____
- [ ] _____
- [ ] _____
- [ ] _____
- [ ] _____
- [ ] _____
- [ ] _____

What Non-profits can you connect with in the Community you serve?

Add your thoughts!

Notes

- [ ] _____

- [ ] _____

- [ ] _____

- [ ] _____

- [ ] _____

- [ ] _____

- [ ] _____

- [ ] _____

Closing Thoughts

As educators we have a duty to give students our best. I am not discrediting any educator who works hard to help produce intelligent, wonderful members of society each day. However, sometimes we do not have all of the tools that we need so that we are at our best, and we may not know it. Other times we know that we do not have these tools, but we are in denial, or we don't bother because of the lack of time. As educators we have to be open-minded to change or enhance our practices, because education is forever changing, and we have to be willing to learn and grow, just as we expect our students to do. Our attitude and the energy that we take on will affect our instructional strategies, the way that we interact with students, and the way that students learn as a whole.

While administrators wear many hats, and they have a wide range of responsibilities, one of their greatness responsibilities is being the pedagogical leader of the school building. They have a duty to fill in gaps that are present in the knowledge of their staff members, regarding instructional practices, through professional development and work sessions. Just as educators have to be open and willing to learn and grow, administrators have to be knowledgeable of new education laws, changes, and ways to stretch their staff so that they deliver high quality instruction to students.

Words to Remember

504 Team

The 504 teams include the school Principal, the parent/guardian, and the general education teacher.

504 Plan

A formal plan that is developed by schools to give students with disabilities the support that they need, and to protect their rights under Section 504 of the Rehabilitation Act.

Accommodations

The change(s) to the learning environment including the equipment that is available, and how assessments/assignments are completed.

Alternative Teaching

The Alternative Co-teaching model is when one educator manages most of the class, and the other educator works in small groups, inside or outside of the classroom.

Apple Classroom

An IOS app designed for iPads that enable teachers to create assignments, projects, and assessment, and transfer files to students.

Authenticity

The quality of being genuine or real.

Class Dojo

A school communication platform that can be used by teachers, students, and families use each day to share what is being learned in the classroom through messages, photos, and videos.

Collaboration

The action of working with other to create or improve something.

Community

A group of people, schools, and businesses that reside in a certain geographical area.

Co-Teaching

When two or more educational professional collaborate and educate students in the same classroom.

Daily 5

A literacy framework that focuses on teaching, learning independence, and building stamina.

Emotional Consistency

The lessening of the intensity of strong emotions, including disappointment and frustrations.

Emotional Intelligence

The ability of people being able to recognize their emotions and the emotions of others, and the ability to use emotional information to guide their behavior and thinking.

Google Classroom

A free web-based service that enable teachers to create assignments, projects, and assessment, and transfer files to students.

IEP Team

Required members of an IEP team include the Intervention Specialist, a general education teacher, a district representative or administrator, and a parent/guardian.

Students who require additional services, such as speech or occupational therapy, will have a Speech and Language Pathologist (SLP), and/or an Occupational Therapist (OT) as members of the IEP team as well.

Inclusive Classroom Environment

A classroom where students with and without disabilities are educated and supported intellectually and academically, according to their needs.

Inclusive Pedagogy

A student-centered approach that contains inclusive practices, and requires the planning of instructional strategies in advance through collaboration, that addresses the various needs of students.

Individualized Education Program (IEP)

IEP stands for individualized educational program, and it is an education plan that is written by the Intervention Specialist (IS), with input from other members of the IEP team. This document contains goals and objectives for the student to master in 1 year minus a day (364 days).

Intervention Specialist (IS)/Interventionist

An educational professional who specializes in providing interventions for students who have been diagnosed with a disability.

Microsoft OneNote

Microsoft OneNote is an online platform that contains notebooks, sections, and pages, that can be used to collaborate with other educators, create lesson plans, edit documents in real time, without needing to be saved.

Modifications

Changes in the content that students are supposed to master.

Occupational Therapist (OT)

An educational professional who focuses on enhancing a child's ability to perform everyday activities and to actively participate in different environments.

One Teach One Support

The One Teach, One Support is a co-teaching model in which one educator is teacher, and the other educator is circulating around the room, assisting and observing students.

Parallel Teaching

The parallel co-teaching model is a co-teaching model in which teachers plan together, and they split the class in half to teach the same content.

Pedagogy

The practice and methods of teaching, and how it influences

learners.

Professional Development (PD)

The process of improving the capabilities of staff through access to education and training opportunities.

Progress Monitoring

The assessment of academic progress, or the lack there of, interventions, and instructional strategies that are put in place to improve student achievement.

Response to Intervention (RTI)

A multi-tired approach to help struggling students by putting interventions in place, and to reveal students who may need to be tested to see if they qualify to receive special education services. A large part of RTI is progress monitoring.

Self-Contained/Single Classroom Environment

A classroom where the Intervention Specialist is responsible for instruction of students who have been diagnosed with having a disability.

Self-Efficacy

How people perceive their abilities to achieve goals

Speech and Language Pathologist (SLP)

An educational professional who is an expert in communication, who provides speech and language services to students who are diagnosed with having a language or speech impediment.

Specially Designed Instruction

Specific instruction that is designed to meet the specific needs of students.

Station Teaching

A co-teaching model in which the instructional content is divided, and the teacher and the interventionist are responsible for teaching different parts of the lesson.

Students with Disabilities (SWD)

Students who have been identified as having physical and/or mental impairments that lead to learning deficits, and/or behavior that impedes their learning, who qualify to receive special education services.

Teacher Based Teams (TBT)

Collaboration sessions where data is shared, and instructional strategies are discussed that include general education teachers, intervention specialists, and administrators such as an Instructional Coach, or Principal.

Teaching Preparation Program

A program designed, at the undergraduate or graduate level, to prepare individuals to be licensed educators.

Team Teaching

A co-teaching model in which both educators are responsible for planning lessons and instructing students.

Time Management

The process planning and organizing, while being conscious of the amount of time being spent on certain activities to increase productivity, efficiency, and effectiveness.

References

Blanton, L. P., Boveda, M., Munoz, L. R., & Pugach, M. C. (2017). The affordances and constraints of special education initial teacher licensure policy for teacher preparation. Teacher Education and Special Education

Driver, M. K., & Murphy, K. M. (2018). Using mixed reality simulations to prepare pre-service special educators for collaboration in inclusive settings. Journal of Technology and Teacher Education, 26(1), 57-77. Retrieved from https://www.learntechlib.org/primary/p/181153

Emmons, C. L., & Zager, D. (2017). Increasing collaboration self-efficacy to improve educational programming for students with autism. Focus on Autism and Other Developmental Disabilities, 33(2), 120-128. https://doi.org/10.1177/1088357616686312

Florian, L. (2017). The heart of inclusive education is collaboration. Pedagogy Studies/Pedagogika, 126(2), 248-253. http://dx.doi.org/ 10.15823/ p.2017.32

Goleman, D. (2015). Emotional intelligence: Why it can matter more than IQ. New York, NY: Bantam: A Division of Random House, Inc.

Juma, S., Lehtomaki, E., & Naukkarinen, A. (2017). Developing inclusive pre-service and in-service teacher education: Insights from Zanzibar Primary School Teachers. International Journal of Whole Schooling, 13(3), 67-87. Retrieved from http://www.wholeschooling.net/Journal_of_Whole_Schooling/articles/13-3%20Juma%20Lehtom%C3%A4ki%20&%20

Naukkarinen %202017.pdf

Juma, S., Lehtomaki, E., & Naukkarinen, A. (2017). Scaffolding teachers to foster inclusive pedagogy and presence through collaborative action research. Educational Action Research, 25(5), 720-736. https://10.1080/09650792.2016.1266957

Kouzes, J.M. & Posner, B.Z. (2017). The leadership challenge. Hoboken, NJ: John Wiley & Sons Inc.

Lemov, D. (2015). Teach like a champion 2.0: 62 techniques that put students on the path to college. San Francisco, CA: Jossey-Bass: A Wiley Brand.

Mintz, J., & Wyse, D. (2015). Inclusive pedagogy and knowledge in special education: Addressing the tension. International Journal of Inclusive Education, 19(11), 1161-1171. https://doi.org/10.1080/13603116. 2015.1044203

Monachino, K. (2018, April, 26). Co-teachingTwo teachers in one class in one class equals success! Extra Credit: The Official Blog of The Ohio Department of Education. https://education.ohio.gov/Media/Extra-Credit-Blog/April-2018/Co-teaching-Two-Teachers-in-One-Class-Equals-Suc

Ohio Department of Education (2010). Credit flexibility guidance: Students with disabilities. Retrieved from http://education.ohio.gov/getattachment/Topics/School-Choice/Credit-Flexibility-Plan/Credit-Flexibility-Guidance-Documents/Students-with-Disabilities.pdf.aspx

Riser-Kositsky, M. (2019, December 17). Special Education: Definition, Statistics, and Trends. Education Week. Retrieved from http://www.edweek.org/ew/issues/special-populations/

RTI Action Network. (2020). What is RTI? National Center for Learning Disabilities. http://www.rtinetwork.org/learn/what

Ruppar, A.L., Neeper, L.S., & Dalsen, J. (2016). Special education teachers perceptions of preparedness to teach students with severe disabilities. Research and Practice for Persons, 41(4), 273-286. https://doi.org/10. 1177/1540796916672843

Shaffer, L., & Thomas-Brown, K. (2015). Enhancing teacher competency through co-teaching and embedded professional development. Journal of Education and Training Studies, 3(3), 117-125. http://dx.doi.org/ 10.11114/jets.v3i3.685

The Academy for Co-teaching and Collaboration. (2013). Co-teaching strategies and examples. Retrieved from https://sites.sju.edu/education/files/2017/05/Co-teaching-definitions-and-examples.pdf

Vollmer, J.R. (2010). Schools Cannot Do It Alone: Building public support for America's public schools. Fairfield, IA: Enlightenment Press.

Yada, A., & Savolainen, H. (2017). Japanese in-service teachers attitudes toward inclusive education and self-efficacy for inclusive practices. Teaching and Teacher Education, 64 (1), 222-229. http://dx.doi.org/10.1016/j.tate.2017.02.005

Zagona, A.L., Kurth, J.A., & MacFarland, S.Z.C. (2017). Teachers views of their preparation for inclusive education and collaboration. Teacher Education & Special Education, 40(3), 163-178. http://doi.org/10.1177/0888406417692969